Discovering Me

Rachel Eastwell

Hillman Publishing

First Paperback edition printed 2015 in the United Kingdom

Published by:
Hillman Publishing
Email: books@hillmanpublishing.co.uk
Web: www.hillmanpublishing.co.uk

ISBN 978-1-909996-09-0

A Catalogue record for this book is available from the British Library.

Typset in 14pt Times New Roman by Hillman Publishing

Hillman Publishing is an imprint of Coastal Peak Ltd

To my beautiful daughters, Susie and Natalie

Contents

Welcome

Sometimes I feel a bit like Alice in Wonderland where she jumps in a rabbit hole and discovers a whole new adventure. In part of that story Alice drinks a potion that makes her shrink and suddenly she has a different view of everything!

Just like Alice I've had the opportunity to look at things in a different way. I have always believed in God but my thoughts and ideas about him have changed a lot since I've grown up. I feel like I've been on quite a journey in my thinking in the last few years, and there are a lot of things that I have discovered that I really wish I'd known when I was younger. I've realised that it's okay to ask questions as you think about who God is. In fact, through this, you may discover that what God thinks about you is a whole lot better than what you first thought.

This book is about you, and I want to invite you to explore your thoughts and discover God for yourself because knowing him is not about believing certain things, but about relationship.

I hope that as I share things that have encouraged me over the last few years they will also encourage you, and that you will enjoy using this book to help you on your own journey of discovery.

There are 30 chapters in this book and so you could do one chapter every day for a month. You might like to read through each chapter with someone else and discuss it with them. If you're doing it on your own you could write down any thoughts, feelings, ideas, dreams or questions you have—because those are all a very important part of your journey.

Your thoughts and feelings count, after all they are part of who you are—and even if they change, that's okay, it's all part of discovering me/you!

There's only one you and you are amazing.

You're chosen and special.

You are beautifully and wonderfully made.

Activity

On a piece of paper or card, in whatever snazzy way you'd like, write the following:

I AM BEAUTIFULLY AND WONDERFULLY MADE!

I AM CHOSEN.

GOD LOVES ME JUST AS I AM!

Use it as a bookmark or even stick it on your mirror so that you can read it often.

Who Am I?

You have been born again, not from a seed that can be destroyed, but through God's everlasting word that can't be destroyed. [1]

When I was a child I really wanted a dog. I used to think about what it would really be like to have a dog and would imagine taking it for walks, playing games with it and snuggling with it when I felt sad. Usually our desires, things we'd like, begin in our thoughts and dreams. Sometimes we end up seeing our dreams come true. In a similar way, I believe we began in the mind of God, that we are his dream come true.

Before time began, God, who is full of Love, imagined sharing his love with us. In the Bible it talks about God the Father, Jesus and the Holy Spirit. They are separate yet one and the same. They form the perfect picture of relationship that God had in mind, the dream of the love that God wanted to share with others.

Even before the world was made God had already chosen us to be His through our union in Christ. [2]

Union means joined together, there is a part of us that comes from God, and God's Holy Spirit reminds us that we belong to him.

A thought, idea or dream can be the start of something, it holds potential for it to become real. The Bible describes God's thought like a seed.

Did you know that some seeds found in frozen soil in Canada were grown and produced flowers? The seeds were thought to be more than 10,000 years old!

Have you ever seen an apple tree produce oranges? No, I didn't think so! Place an apple seed in soil, give it water and light, and it has all the potential within it to produce an apple tree. An apple seed will always produce an apple tree, a pear seed will always produce a pear tree, and so on.

In the same way that a seed has everything it needs to grow and develop, you have everything you need to grow and develop in the image and likeness of God, because that is how you were created. Everything that is true about God is true about you and although you may not always see it, the potential is in you.

Knowing God helps you to know yourself, to see yourself as God sees you.

Jesus was God but also human, just like you. Jesus is described as the light of man. What does a light do? It shows what is there; Jesus came to show what you look like. Jesus reveals the real you.

Activity

Draw a tree with some fruit on it and on the fruit write some words that describe Jesus, if you're stuck take a look in Galatians 5 in a Bible.

Remember these words also describe how God sees you.

Who Is Jesus?

I am the light of the world. Whoever follows me will never walk in darkness, but will have the light of life. [3]

Have you ever wondered why some people mentioned in the Bible, had a hard time accepting Jesus and didn't believe he was who he said he was? Could it be that because so many of them had a wrong understanding of who God was, and that this Jesus—who was friends with bad people, and mixed with the sick and other weirdoes, was totally unlike the God they thought they knew? Surely he couldn't have been the son of God that they had imagined? Jesus acted differently to how they expected the son of God to act. They based their ideas on the God they thought they knew.

For example there was confusion in Luke 9:52-56, when Jesus and his followers were on their way to a village but the people didn't want them there, so the followers turned to Jesus and said, *"Lord, should we call down fire from heaven to destroy them?"* Jesus strongly disagreed with this and told them that he did not come to destroy men but to save them;

yet this was probably the kind of God they would have heard and read about from their own families and culture.

Jesus came to reveal God's love for man. He is described as light and a light reveals what is hidden in the darkness.

> *The Life-Light was the real thing:*
> *Every person entering Life*
> *he brings into Light.*
> *He was in the world,*
> *the world was there through him,*
> *and yet the world didn't even notice.*
> *He came to his own people,*
> *but they didn't want him.*
> *But whoever did want him,*
> *who believed he was who he claimed*
> *and would do what he said,*
> *he made to be their true selves,*
> *their child-of-God selves.* [4]

You might get confused by some things you hear about God, but look at the way Jesus dealt with people and the stories he told, because he was and is exactly the same as God. Jesus demonstrated God's true love for man. Jesus revealed his true self, a child of God just like us.

Activity

Unscramble the words to find out what else Jesus came to reveal.

TAHT DOG EDMA SHI MEHO NI SU.

What Is God Really Like?

*Jesus said "Anyone who has seen me has seen the Father." * [5]

If we want to know what God is really like then we can look at Jesus, because Jesus is the perfect mirror of God's character. We can read about Jesus and see what he was like, how he treated people and what he did. Jesus loved people; he forgave them and healed their sicknesses. Let's take a closer look at some examples of how Jesus treated people when he was here on earth.

In the story of Zacchaeus we are told about a man who wasn't liked by many people, he collected taxes from them and probably cheated them by taking more money than he should have. One day Zacchaeus learns that Jesus will be visiting the town where he lives. He wants to see Jesus, but so does everyone else and there are crowds of people. To get a better view, Zacchaeus climbs up a tree.

When Jesus sees Zacchaeus, he tells him to get down from the tree because he wants to go to his house. Zacchaeus is so pleased that Jesus wants to visit him, but the people around complain and question why Jesus is visiting a bad person like Zacchaeus, who doesn't deserve such an honour. Guess what happens next?

Jesus, who is exactly like God, doesn't judge Zacchaeus and tell him off for cheating people. He's friendly and kind towards him. Zacchaeus probably felt very special, to think that this man Jesus who he'd heard so much about, was coming to his house. We see from this story that Jesus' act of friendship caused the man to change his ways.

Zacchaeus stood up and said to the Lord, "Listen, sir! I will give half my belongings to the poor, and if I have cheated anyone, I will pay back four times as much." [6]

Jesus made Zacchaeus feel good about himself, because he loved him. In God's eyes we are worth so much to him. When we see ourselves that way it causes us to act that way too. The way we think about ourselves affects the way we behave.

The second example I want to give you of how Jesus treated people and what God is really like, is in the healing of a man who was lowered through the roof of a house. [7]

In those days, it was often thought that if someone was sick, it was because of some bad thing that he had done. So when Jesus said to the man, *"Your sins are forgiven"*, the religious people were annoyed. Jesus also healed the man and demonstrated that God is a God who forgives and heals, not a God who puts sickness on people to teach them a lesson.

Jesus revealed that some of the ideas people had about God were wrong, even people who had read a lot about God, like the religious people, had got it so wrong they didn't even recognise Jesus as the Son of God.

Activity

Draw a little cartoon picture of the Zaccheus story and the faces of the people in the crowd, when Jesus talks to him.

Holy Spirit

'God's spirit joins himself with our spirits to declare that we are God's children.' [8]

God has been misunderstood throughout history, and not everything you hear or read about him is true. It doesn't matter how clever the person who said it may be, or how well they know the Bible, everyone has their own opinion and ideas about God.

You might be thinking 'well that's confusing! How do I know who is right and who is wrong?' God has given us his spirit, his way of thinking. The Holy Spirit is described in the Bible as a helper, teacher or comforter who guides us into all the truth about who God really is.

Have your friends ever told you about someone, a teacher at school, for example, how bad they are, or how strict and mean they are, but when you finally get to know that teacher for yourself you discover s/he wasn't at all like s/he described!

We can know about someone and yet not really know them. We can make judgements about people that we have heard about but not really got to know for ourselves. Judgement basically means to make a decision, and it's difficult to make a decision about someone or something based on other people's opinions. You can only truly begin to make a decision about something when you've experienced it for yourself.

This is what God invites you to do; in fact he loves it when you do. In the Bible it says 'Taste and see that God is good.'[9]

We can hear plenty of things about God, from our parents, friends, TV, books, church and the Bible but it is only through close friendship with God that we can really know him.

Think about the last time you had a really good time with a friend or relation, or think about the last time someone said something to you that made you feel really good inside. God has this to offer you all the time.

We can look to other people for these kinds of feelings and that's fine, but those feelings can come and go. God invites you to meet with him every day to experience his 'crazy for you' love! This is why he created you because he has so much love that he has to share it and you are the object of his love!

By God's spirit you can hear his thoughts towards you, they will always be encouraging, lovely and positive thoughts. Get into the habit of this and you'll find yourself doing it a lot because his thoughts towards us are so good!

Activity

Circle true or false about these things:

God likes me and loves me	True False
Sometimes God is in a bad mood with me	True False
I never disappoint God	True False
Jesus only mixed with people that were 'good'	True False

The Bible

No one has ever seen God. The only Son, who is the same as God and is at the Father's side, he has made him known. [10]

Now, if you're familiar with the Bible then you might be thinking: Hold on a minute what about some of these stories where God is angry with people? In the story of Noah, it tells us that God wiped out all of mankind because they were so bad and he only rescued Noah and his family; or the story of Moses where we hear that all kinds of horrible plagues and events were sent by God on the Egyptians.

In the past I have often struggled to try and understand some of the things written in the Bible, especially as I've got to know God's love more, and I've found it hard to understand what is written there about God. Although it is quite difficult, let me share with you some of the things that have helped in my understanding.

People can have different ideas and opinions about things. Two people might witness an event and, if we read their stories, they might tell similar but different accounts of what happened.

In early times people were trying to make sense of their world and of who God is; there were all kinds of stories, passed on in families and societies to try and explain things that happened in the world. Even now when disasters happen, like earthquakes, tsunamis and wars, people are always asking questions, wanting to know why it happened.

The Bible is a wonderful book written by different people, based on their experiences and how they saw God. Often, in a good book, you have different voices, or characters contributing to the story, and it is not until the end that it all makes sense. In the same way, the Bible tells the people's story of who they think God is, and the great ending to the story is Jesus, who is God in human form, speaking with God's voice. Jesus shows what God is really like.

When you read the Bible and you see love shown, you know it is God's voice speaking.

Activity

Colour in the speech bubbles that you think speak in God's voice of love and leave blank the speech bubbles you think might be what someone thinks God might be saying.

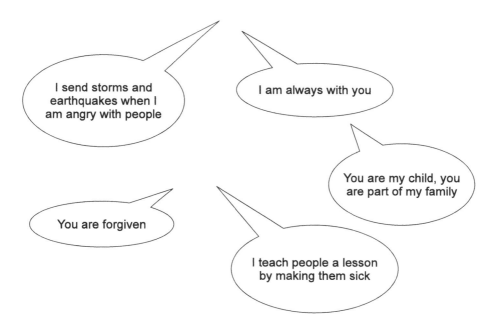

The Original Recipe

God's whole nature is living in Christ in human form. Because you belong to Christ, you have been made complete.[11]

Adam and Eve are the first humans talked about in the Bible. The story in Genesis tells us that God created them to be like himself but they were tempted to think they weren't like God and they felt they needed to *become* like him. When God came looking for them in the garden they ran and hid and felt ashamed because they hadn't believed God. In *trying* to be like him, they felt separated from him.

However when Adam and Eve hid in the Garden, God was there, always loving them, and he never lost sight of them or thought any less of them. I hope this little story helps to illustrate this:

There was once a recipe for a cake, a really amazing cake, but the recipe goes missing. It gets put down somewhere and forgotten, but no one's too bothered; there's lots of other ways to make amazing cakes. They don't really need the original recipe anyway, they can make as good a cake themselves, or so they thought. However the cake recipe gets changed slightly each time it's made and doesn't quite match the original. People try to make it look and taste as good as the original and even add some extra toppings to cover it up, but it's just not the same.

Thankfully, the original cake recipe has never been forgotten by the master baker and he never loses sight of what the cake truly looked and tasted like. The original cake appears one day and people see and taste the cake for themselves and it reminds them of what the cake was always meant to be like. People are so glad that the missing cake recipe is found again and the chef is delighted as he sees cakes appearing everywhere, true to the original recipe.

Even though people might forget who they are and to whom they belong, God sent Jesus so that they could be found; Jesus restores us to the original recipe from which we were made. God has always known us as his children. He made us in his likeness, and his plan for our lives is to discover that identity. We have always belonged to God. In seeing him as our Father God, we find our original selves and we change our thinking about who we are. We see that we are just like him.

Activity

```
U A R E D T K Y O S I I C E E
N V E A M Z T D T S U H I T T
S S E L E M A L B I I G E H U
N S A C V C L K P L T L H N P
E I W Z O N L I D E P N I T L
V G C A M A R O B M R O E G E
I W O Q V U F K O O N F Q D U
G C M M Y G B C F R I G E X I
R H E H O V A L U A B L E C F
O O X D T C I D D T K O I D T
F S O M U M R R S J H L U D E
E E L U P C R S L E X U X O H
A N K B D U L V M F D J G V R
Y J H E Y C Y U T A P A R Q V
```

BLAMELESS

CHILDOFGOD

CHOSEN

COMPLETE

FORGIVEN

IDENTITY

PERFECT

UNION

VALUABLE

The Lost Son

God's kindness makes you change your mind

Let's look at the father in this story from Luke, Jesus told this story to show what God is like.

Jesus went on to say, "There was once a man who had two sons. The younger one said to him, 'Father, give me my share of the property now.' So the man divided his property between his two sons. After a few days, the younger son sold his part of the property and left home with the money. He went to a country far away, where he wasted his money in reckless living. He spent everything he had. Then a severe famine spread over that country, and he was left without a thing. So he went to work for one of the citizens of that country, who sent him out to his farm to take care of the pigs. He wished he could fill himself with the bean pods the pigs ate, but no one gave him anything to eat. At last he came to his senses and said, 'All my father's hired workers have more than they can eat, and here I am about to starve! I will get up and go to my father and say, "Father, I have sinned against God and against you. I am no longer fit to be called your son; treat me as one of your hired workers."' So he got up and started back to his father.

"He was still a long way from home when his father saw him; his heart was filled with pity, and he ran, threw his arms around his son, and kissed him. 'Father,' the son said, 'I have sinned against God and against you. I am no longer fit to be called your son.' But the father called to his servants. 'Hurry!' he said. 'Bring the best robe and put it on him. Put a ring on his finger and shoes on his feet. Then go and get the prize calf and kill it, and let us celebrate with a feast! For this son of mine was dead, but now he is alive; he was lost, but now he has been found.' And so the feasting began. [12]

The father is waiting for his son to return and is confident that his love for him will bring him home. He is looking forward to seeing him and waiting to give him a hug. Our Father God is confident that as we experience his love for us, we will come back for more.

Knowing and experiencing God's love for us is so enjoyable. He loves us and enjoys hanging out with us so much that we cannot help but love and enjoy him back. His eye is always on us. He is always thinking about us and loves to be with us and within us. We are so precious to him. He adores us. We can see this in the story by the way the father receives his son, running towards him, greeting him with such a great hug. Then to top it all, there's a welcoming party, new clothes, a ring, food and friends. Wow, and all this after he had wasted his father's money.

You might not have such a good relationship with your own father but I hope you might be able to imagine through this story how much God loves you. His love for us is pictured so beautifully here. It's not about how good, clever or successful we are and has nothing to do with what we can do for him, but it is everything to do with what we mean to him.

He values us so greatly for whom we are. We are special. We are his children.

Activity

Draw a cartoon of the father welcoming the son back home.

The Misunderstood Dad

'My son,' the father answered, 'you are always here with me, and everything I have is yours. [13]

The next part of this story is about the other son, the older brother who is struggling with all that has just happened.

"In the meantime the older son was out in the field. On his way back, when he came close to the house, he heard the music and dancing. So he called one of the servants and asked him, 'What's going on?' [7] *'Your brother has come back home,' the servant answered, 'and your father has killed the prize calf, because he got him back safe and sound.' The older brother was so angry that he would not go into the house; so his father came out and begged him to come in. But he spoke back to his father, 'Look, all these years I have worked for you like a slave, and I have never disobeyed your orders. What have you given me? Not even a goat for me to have a feast with my friends! But this son*

of yours wasted all your property on prostitutes, and when he comes back home, you kill the prize calf for him!' 'My son,' the father answered, 'you are always here with me, and everything I have is yours. But we had to celebrate and be happy, because your brother was dead, but now he is alive; he was lost, but now he has been found.'" [14]

The older brother is having a hard time accepting the father's love. He can only see the unfairness of it all and is tormented by the fact that his brother got so much love and attention when he had done nothing to deserve it. He, on the other hand, worked hard but felt like he had nothing in return. The older brother feels rejected and unloved even though it is far from the truth. He has misunderstood his father.

The father gently explains to him that he has never left him. He has always been loved and everything was already his. He too did not have to do anything to earn his father's love and acceptance. The only thing stopping this son from enjoying his Father's love was his own thinking.

Activity

How was the older brother feeling?

Was the brother trying to please his father by living right; how do we know that?

The brother had misunderstood his father; in your own words describe the father's love for his sons.

Lost

*Know that the L*ORD *is God. He made us, and we belong to him. We are his people. We are the sheep belonging to his flock.* [15]

In the story of the lost son it's not that the boy got lost and couldn't find his way home, but rather he got lost in his thinking. He lost sight of the fact that he was a son, and that he belonged to a father who loved him.

In these two stories, the owners of the sheep and the coin set out to find them because obviously the coin and the sheep cannot do anything themselves to be found. When they are found, the owners celebrate, because just like the father in the story of the lost son they are so pleased to have found what was lost.

The lost son didn't get found in the same way. In this story we see how the son 'comes to his senses'. He has a light bulb moment—'ding'—changes his mind and realises that he would be better off returning home where he belongs and where there is love. He is found when he changes his thinking about whom he is—a son—and where he came from: A home with a loving father, a good man who even treated his workers well. As he's reminded about these truths he is drawn back to where he belongs and on returning home he receives far more love than he ever hoped for.

The lost son, the lost coin and the lost sheep were all lost in different ways. They were all helpless, but because their owners were so attached to them they were eventually found.

God used Jesus to help us see that we belong, to show us who we are: God's children, and where we come from: A good God, so that we too can change our thinking and realise that he has always been with us. We have always been loved and nothing needs to be done to earn his love and acceptance, we can only come to our senses and discover that he has always loved us.

He celebrates when we realise and enjoy his love for us.

Activity

Read the story of the lost coin and lost sheep in the Bible in Luke 15, and write down any thoughts you might have about these stories and how they describe what God is like.

Royal Thoughts

You are what you think! [16]

We all have good days and bad days, but the good thing is that God doesn't just love you because of the good things you do that day or what you've done or haven't done. He loves you for who you are. Maybe there are things about yourself you wish you could change, maybe there are things you wish you could do, or maybe you have dreams of doing something amazing one day. God knows your every thought and he believes in you. He sees the best in you. He sees you living out your dreams. The more we see ourselves as God sees us, the more we live out the best in us and fulfil our dreams.

Why is it so important to think about how we see ourselves? God has designed us to live this way, he wants us to live life to the full; it's his pleasure and delight to see us living out our lives while feeling and experiencing peace, joy and love.

Think of a King, a king who rules over a country. If he's an angry, bad tempered king, his kingdom probably isn't a very happy place to live, and the people there probably don't enjoy life much, because of the way he runs the kingdom. However if the king is a happy, good tempered person then the kingdom is most likely a very good place to live, and the happy influence he has over the country makes it a more enjoyable place for people to live.

In the same way that a king has power over a country and influences it, the way you think has the power to have an effect on your life; so if you think good and happy thoughts you are more likely to have a good and happy life.

We are sons and daughters of our father God, the most High King, and he leads the way for us to walk as royalty, leading good lives. As we realise his good opinion of us: that we are pleasing in his sight and that we are his work of art, his masterpiece, we can enjoy living a life with peace and confidence.

Activity

Write down some good thoughts you can think about. Here are some to get you started:

Thank you that even when I fail, you still love me.

Thank you that even though I might feel rubbish, you can't stop thinking how amazing I am!

Thank you that I am your work of art!

Thank you that your banner over me is LOVE!

Delight Yourself

Delight yourself in the Lord and he will give you the desires of your heart. [17]

The word delight from this verse in the Bible also means to pamper yourself. Pampering means different things to different people. Some might enjoy having a massage, or being waited-on, perhaps being served with food and drinks, or maybe just relaxing and enjoying yourself. God wants you to enjoy yourself with him and to pamper yourself through him. He loves it when you rest in him.

Praying doesn't have to be boring, praying is a conversation where not only do you talk to God, but you listen to what he has to say. You can also just take time to think about the thoughts God has about you and enjoy those thoughts. Imagine yourself in your favourite place, somewhere relaxing, on a beach or by a beautiful lake, and imagine him saying those things to you. Imagine yourself listening to those good thoughts that he has about you until you feel well and truly pampered.

One of the books in the Bible is written by a man called John, and he describes himself as the disciple whom Jesus loved [18]. Some might think that's a bit big-headed of him but maybe he was actually reminding himself and being delighted in God's love and acceptance of him.

In the second part of the verse, God gives us the desires of our hearts. As we build our friendship with God we will find that the good things we hope for come our way. As we share our dreams with him, he shows us the way to fulfil those dreams.

Activity

One way you might like to begin building your friendship with God is to ask God to help you feel his love and then to take a verse from the Bible and allow your imagination to picture it in your mind. Think about the verse for a few minutes with your eyes closed.

Try it with this verse:

> *The Lord is my shepherd;*
> *I have all that I need.*
> *He lets me rest in green meadows;*
> *he leads me beside peaceful streams,* [19]

Draw a picture of what came to your mind and write down any thoughts you had.

Looking Up

Don't worry about anything; instead, pray about everything. Tell God what you need, and thank him for all he has done.[20]

Have you ever heard people say when they are climbing a ladder or on some high place, "Don't look down." It's so true; when we look down we can lose our focus and get fearful as we realise how high up we are.

The Bible tells us of a time when Jesus had been speaking to a crowd and they were getting hungry. He loved the people and wanted to provide food for them. The situation would have looked difficult; there were so many people, yet so little food, all they had were a few loaves and some fish but Jesus looked to his Father God in heaven and believed he would supply what they needed. He let his thoughts focus on his Father God's love and care rather than on the difficult situation.

What we spend time thinking about really affects how we feel.

There's a story in the Bible that always fascinates me. It's where Jesus and his followers got into a boat to cross to the other side of the lake, suddenly there's a storm and the followers are panicking, but Jesus is asleep in the boat! Jesus had such peace of mind that he could sleep during a storm in the middle of the lake. The same is possible for you, too.

There are times in our lives when things can make us feel afraid, especially when we keep thinking about those things and wondering what might happen. We worry. Worrying is when you spend time thinking the worst about a situation in your life, and you usually end up feeling pretty bad. Instead, try to spend some time thinking about the good things that could happen and imagine how much God loves you and cares about you; this way, you can end up feeling good inside and feeling calm when everyone around you is panicking.

"I tell you, do not worry. Don't worry about your life and what you will eat or drink. And don't worry about your body and what you will wear. Isn't there more to life than eating? Aren't there more important things for the body than clothes?"

"Look at the birds of the air. They don't plant or gather crops. They don't put away crops in storerooms. But your Father who is in heaven feeds them. Aren't you worth much more than they are?

"Can you add even one hour to your life by worrying? [21]

Jesus reminds us that even the birds get fed, and we are much more valuable to him than the birds, he will look after us so much more.

Activity

If you are going through a difficult time with something, remember that Jesus is looking after you and write down a thank you for that situation getting sorted.

Nothing Can Separate You From God's Love

Then Jesus said, "Come to me, all of you who are weary and carry heavy burdens, and I will give you rest. [22]

When I was about 10 years old I remember becoming quite anxious about friendships and I'd have good and bad days at school. I thought that if I was good and did good things then God would help me through my day and that I'd have a good day. I had ideas of what good and bad things were, such as helping at home, would gain me points. But the down side to this thinking was that when I lied, or said things I shouldn't, then I thought God was in a bad mood with me. I felt that I needed to grovel and hope that God would at least forgive me, but I certainly did not think there was any chance that he would help me after that kind of behaviour. I thought he must be cross with me, especially when I did the same bad things week after week. I spent many years with this kind of thinking and I didn't enjoy it much!

Sometimes, when something you believed turns out to not actually be true, it's such a relief! I remember when years later I discovered that this idea about God I'd had wasn't actually true at all. It was like a huge load had been lifted from my shoulders and for quite some time afterwards I felt as though I was floating.

God wants us to come to him no matter what. He wants nothing to get in the way of his relationship with us. Even when we feel as though we don't deserve his love, that is not how he feels about us. He loves us unconditionally. The only thing that can get in the way of him loving us is what we think about him, like the incorrect thoughts I had about him.

In Luke 10 there's a story about Mary and Martha, who

were expecting a visit from Jesus. Martha was so busy trying to make everything right for Jesus that she missed out on enjoying his company. Mary, on the other hand, sat down and listened to all that he had to say. Martha was annoyed at her sister for not helping but Jesus told her that Mary had made the right choice. She should not worry but simply chill out with him.

How can something separate you from God's love when you are united with him? Martha only missed out because she was distracted with other things rather than being aware of Jesus's presence.

Activity

Take a piece of card about 10cm x 5cm and fold it in half. Put the card in front of you so that the fold is at the top. Draw a small self-portrait on one side and on the other get a felt tip pen and draw a big heart that fills the space. Place the top of a pencil just inside the card and tape it into the middle of the card so that both sides of the card are secure. Then hold the bottom of the pencil and roll it in between both of your hands very quickly. What do you see?

Enjoy chilling out with him, enjoy the good things in life and be thankful.

God Is Not Distant

'Let us give thanks to the God and Father of our Lord Jesus Christ! For in our union with Christ he has blessed us by giving us every spiritual blessing in the heavenly world. Even before the world was made, God had already chosen us to be his through our union with Christ, so that we would be holy and without fault before him.

Because of his love God had already decided that through Jesus Christ he would make us his children—this was his pleasure and purpose. Let us praise God for his glorious grace, for the free gift he gave us in his dear Son! For by the blood of Christ we are set free, that is, our sins are forgiven. How great is the grace of God, which he gave to us in such large measure!' [23]

Jesus demonstrates how close God is to us. Man has often thought that God is far away and distant and to be searched for, and very often the search is in the wrong place. The Bible speaks a lot about the kingdom of God and that it's not up there in the sky but Jesus says:

'The kingdom of God is within you.' [24]

What does that mean?

The way God works, is through us. God showed us the truth about what he is really like when he became a man, Jesus. God is love and Jesus demonstrated that love. In the same way that God worked in Jesus, he works in and through us. It may not always be evident because we have often misunderstood God and not seen ourselves the way God sees us, but the treasure is in us. God is in us!

In the Bible, there is a story about a field in which there is a hidden treasure. We are like that field. God knows the hidden treasure within us, he knows our value and he went to great lengths to find us. Not only that, but it gives him great pleasure and joy to have done so.

Activity

Unscramble these words that describe you:

SLEMBASEL   TPECEDCA   VODLE

LUAVLBAE   REFTCEP   LICHD FO DGO

Psalm 139 Part 1

Lord, you have examined me and you know me.
You know everything I do;
from far away you understand all my thoughts.
You see me, whether I am working or resting;
you know all my actions.
Even before I speak,
you already know what I will say.
You are all around me on every side;
you protect me with your power.
Your knowledge of me is too deep;
it is beyond my understanding.

Where could I go to escape from you?
Where could I get away from your presence?
If I went up to heaven, you would be there;
if I lay down in the world of the dead, you would be there.
If I flew away beyond the east
or lived in the farthest place in the west,
you would be there to lead me,
you would be there to help me.
I could ask the darkness to hide me
or the light around me to turn into night,
but even darkness is not dark for you,
and the night is as bright as the day.
Darkness and light are the same to you.

You created every part of me;
you put me together in my mother's womb.
I praise you because you are to be feared;
all you do is strange and wonderful.

I know it with all my heart. ²⁵

What a beautiful Psalm that describes Father God's relationship with us: So close that we cannot hide from him, no matter where we may end up or whatever we may do. He never leaves us even in our darkest moments. I love to imagine parts of this psalm, that his arm is around me and that he's whispering these words to me, that I am his beloved. I've begun to realise more and more that God is so close to us because he is part of us; this psalm makes me think of that.

In some versions of the Bible it says *'He knit me together in my mother's womb,'* and I imagine something that's been knitted and has many different threads woven together to make something lovely. His love and life have been knitted together with us.

Activity

Pick a part of this Psalm and write it out, and think about why you like it. Think about it before you go to sleep to-night.

Psalm 139 Part 2

When my bones were being formed,
carefully put together in my mother's womb,
when I was growing there in secret,
you knew that I was there—
you saw me before I was born.
The days allotted to me
had all been recorded in your book,
before any of them ever began.
O God, how precious are your thoughts toward me;
how many of them there are!
If I counted them, they would be more than the grains of
sand.
When I awake, I am still with you. [26]

When we think about where we come from, our first thought is our parents, our family, but when we look further than that we discover that we were in God's mind even before we existed. Even before we were born God had us in mind. We come from him. We are special because we were God's idea from the very beginning. He thinks so much of us, and this has never changed.

You might think: Well if we come from God, and God is good, why are we not always good? In fact we can look at the world around us and think that people sometimes behave pretty badly.

It's hard to behave in a way that is opposite to how you see yourself; if you think you are bad it's hard to try and be good, because we usually act the way we think. To be able to live right, or to be good, we need to start by seeing who we really are. We need to realise our true identity—to see that we come from God.

As we discover who we are, and that we are so valuable in God's mind, we will begin to feel valued and loved. This Psalm describes how loved we are. God can't stop thinking about us, and that must mean that he likes us a lot! His thoughts about us are more numerous than the sands and as we think about how God feels about us we become more like him.

When we live out of our true identity it also helps us in the way we view those around us, we appreciate their value more as we realise how God loved each and every one of us from the very beginning.

Activity

Write down the names of some people you appreciate and why?

Thank God for them.

Reflect

So all of us who have had that veil removed can see and reflect the glory of the Lord. [27]

To think about something a lot is sometimes known as reflecting. The word 'reflect' means to look back at something. This is interesting because when I hear the word reflect I think of a mirror. When you look in the mirror and you see yourself, you see what you look like.

Perhaps you wish you had a different hairstyle or were taller. Imagine if you went up to a mirror to look at yourself and the reflection you saw was what you'd wished for! The wonderful thing about God's thoughts towards us is that they reflect who we really are; it's not just wishful thinking. As we look and think about God and see his love, joy, peace and patience toward us we discover that this is also a reflection of what he sees in us!

Have you ever seen one of those make-over shows where they decorate a room, or transform a house or garden from a mess to something wonderful? The owners return home at the end of the show and when they open their eyes, they are so amazed at the transformation!

I used to think that I could transform myself through trying harder to be a better person; I'd make plans on how to improve myself, like to not lie or to be more helpful, or to pray more but then when my plans failed I was disappointed and I felt bad about myself again. It was always wishful thinking and never a reality.

I only felt amazement when my eyes were opened and I discovered how God felt about me, that he saw me as blameless and innocent right from the very beginning. It wasn't a makeover at all, it was how I looked all along, but I could not see it. Jesus came to reveal the truth about us.

Activity

Unscramble the words to write a truth about you.

SUSJE HOSWS EM THAW I KLOO KILE, I
FETLECR MIH.

Love Wins

The grass withers and the flowers fall, but the word of our God endures forever. [28]

This verse has given me hope at times in my life when I felt that things weren't going as I'd like them to and at times when I've struggled with disappointments.

As I've learned more about how big God's love is towards us, this verse has come to mean even more. I believe that the 'word of our God' part of the verse means his love. I picture his love as a flowing river, because nothing can stop a river flowing. If you've ever been caught in the current of a river you'll know that it's strong and powerful: just like God's love; it never stops flowing. The river will continue to flow to its destination even though it might take many turns to get there.

God's love never fails. God cannot stop loving his children. Love is who he is and he cannot deny himself.

God's love is powerful and strong but not in a forceful way; it just keeps flowing and having its influence. It reminds me of the fable of the sun and the wind. In this fable the sun and the wind have a competition to see who can remove a man's coat. The wind thinks it is so strong it can force the coat off the man. However, the sun knows that gentleness will win. Under the gentle influence of the sun's warmth, the man eventually does take his coat off. He wasn't forced or controlled by the sun; he didn't have to take his coat off, but he does so because of the influence of the sun.

It is the same way with God's love. When we experience and feel God's love for us, it affects the way we feel about ourselves (we actually *feel* loved), it also influences the way we act and the way we feel about other people.

God's way is never to force people against their will but rather to win people over with his love!

Activity

Think of a word to describe God's kind of love beginning with each letter here

L

O

V

E

Love Is Gentle

My teaching will fall like drops of rain and form on the earth like dew.
My words will fall like showers on young plants, like gentle rain on tender grass. [29]

God is so gentle with us. He cares for us, and it is through this care that we grow and develop into our own beautiful personalities.

There may be things about yourself that you want to change or you may get frustrated by things in your life that you struggle with. Maybe there are friendships or family relationships where you find yourself saying things you wish you hadn't. Perhaps you feel under pressure to act a certain way and you end up doing things you regret because you are afraid of what people might think of you.

Father God is not interested in changing you, or making you into something you don't want to be. His longing is to reveal to you your value and your worth. You have always been in God's mind.

Imagine you want to grow some strawberries in your garden. You buy a young strawberry plant in a small pot and instead of planting it, you tell it every week that it should be growing strawberries. After all, if it is a strawberry plant it *should* act like one. I don't think it will develop much fruit this way, but if you find out how to care for the plant and plant it in good soil, look after it, feed and water it, then, given time, you will see fruit growing. It won't have to try and be a strawberry plant; fruit will grow given the right conditions. In the same way the more we hear and think about what God believes about us, the more our true selves, who God meant us to be, will show.

This is God's plan for us: as he loves and cares for us, we discover all that he has planted within us.

Activity

Draw two trees. Label one tree the tree of knowing good and evil and write on it some rules for living right; for example I must not lie, I must share etc. Label the other tree the Jesus tree and write your name in the middle and underneath list some things which God believes true about you, for example: I am kind, I am generous etc.

Out Of The Darkness

'In him we live and move and exist.' It is as some of your poets have said, 'We too are his children.'[30]

From some of the stories we've read or heard about in the Bible we can see that people thought that God was separate from people: a big distant God in the sky looking down on them, watching for when they were bad and ready to punish them. This kind of thinking began in the Garden of Eden, in the story of Adam and Eve.

The truth is though, that God has always been close to us and wants to express himself through us. This has always been God's plan right from the beginning.

Jesus came to reveal how close he actually was! He came to remind us of who we are. Jesus turned on the light so that we can now see who God really is and how we come from him.

The movie 'The Croods' is about a prehistoric family who stay in their dark cave and follow the rules because they think they should keep away from life outside. Then one day the daughter sees a light shining into the cave and decides to go out and see where the light is coming from. As she does so, she meets Guy who, to cut a long story short, leads the Croods out of the dark and into the light. Guy introduces them to a way of life that was there all along but they just didn't know it. This was what Jesus came to do, to show us a way of life, a way of knowing God that was there all along but we just didn't know it.

Light shines in the darkness and reveals what was there all along. People forgot who God really was until Jesus came to reveal him. Jesus showed that God is so close to us; in finding him we find ourselves and we discover our true selves.

Jesus said this to his followers, just before his death:

When that day comes, you will know that I am in my Father and that you are in me, just as I am in you. [31]

We were made to reflect his light and life.

Activity

Write God, Jesus and the Holy Spirit in the above symbol and your own name in the middle; this is how much you are wrapped up in him.

You've Already Got It

Arise, shine, for your light has come, and the glory of the LORD rises upon you. [32]

Just like the Croods, we can get the wrong impression about things and live in the dark. In a sense the Croods were imprisoned by their own thoughts. The truth is God loves you and thinks you are amazing, knowing this truth brings freedom, freedom to be yourself.

We too can think that we have to act a certain way or be something we are not, and as long as we think we are not a good person, we will keep chasing after that thing. This is a bit like a dog chasing its own tail! The dog goes round and round in circles trying to bite its own tail without realising that the tail actually belongs to the dog and that it is a part of him!

When we chase after things that we think are out there, trying to please others or trying hard to be perfect, we can end up going round in circles; we can get stressed, worn out and feel trapped. However, when we realize that we have been made perfect and that this is how God sees us, we begin to reflect that opinion. It's much easier to live knowing who you are than trying to get hold of something that seems out of reach.

When you know how God feels about you, it brings peace and calm to your life, and everything else in life is easier when you feel calm.

Have you heard the old story of the ugly duckling? He was very sad because he looked different to all the other ducklings. Then one day he saw some beautiful swans and he wanted to join them. As he swam over to them, he saw in the waters' reflection that he himself had grown into a beautiful swan. He was a swan all along but didn't know it until he saw the truth in the mirror.

The truth is that God loves you and delights in you! Knowing this truth brings freedom; freedom to be yourself.

Activity

Get a piece a paper to stick on your mirror, or make a book-mark and write on it using some nice pens, the following.

Everyday in everyway God's life inside me is making my life better and better.

Perfect Love

*There is no fear in love; perfect love drives out all fear.
So then, love has not been made perfect in anyone who is
afraid, because fear has to do with punishment.* [33]

Fear comes when you feel that you have let someone down and so you cannot speak to them. Fear comes when you feel as though you haven't done enough to make someone happy. Fear comes when you feel you have to do certain things in order to be accepted; when you feel you need to act in a certain way to please someone. Then sometimes, that can lead to lying because you cannot be truly yourself.

When I first started in high school one of my so-called friendships was based on fear. Sometimes I would feel so scared that I would deliberately miss the bus or a couple of times I faked feeling ill so that I wouldn't have to go to school and face the fear. At that time the feeling of fear was much greater than the feeling that God loved me!

It's interesting that in the Bible 'Fear not' or 'Do not be

afraid' is said some 365 times. People in the Bible were very often afraid of God so it is no wonder it needed to be said so many times! Jesus came to drive out that fear through showing perfect love, a perfect picture of God.

God's love is perfect. It is complete, not lacking anything. There are no missing pieces that you have to fill. There are no 'buts' with God. He does not say 'well I love you, but…!' He does not expect anything from you. He only loves you. God is love!

That is why his love drives out all fear. With God you don't need to feel that you owe him something. Perfect love doesn't love in order to get something back. Rather God loves you so much that you cannot help but respond, like when someone smiles at you and you cannot help but smile back.

Love is hard to resist. You might act nice towards someone even if you don't like them, because you're afraid of them; of what they might do to you. But when someone shows love to you unconditionally and you have a good relationship with them, it is much harder to act in a bad way around them because you love them!

Activity

Think about any fears you might have, it might be something that you want to do but you feel that you can't do it. Fill in the gaps and make this your prayer.

Thank you God that even though I feel _____, you are always with me and that I can do anything with your strength.

I picture myself doing/being _____.

God Is love

Love is patient and kind; it is not jealous or conceited or proud; love is not ill-mannered or selfish or irritable; love does not keep a record of wrongs; [34]

These verses in Corinthians describe what love is. Since we know that God is love, we can replace the word 'love' here, with the word 'God'.

God is so patient with us; he isn't drumming his fingers, wondering how many times he has to put up with our mistakes—no, he doesn't get annoyed easily at all! God is not demanding or moody or disappointed in you, he always believes in you and is so happy that he sings over you.

In school and society we are quick to label people for example 'he's a naughty boy' or 'she's a gossip.' This is what we believe about them, but does that identify who they really are?

God is love and that is his identity. It is who he is and so he naturally is all those things described in the verse at the start of this chapter. When you get things wrong people label you, and you might label yourself a failure, but God knows that the things we do don't define who we are. It's not that he pretends not to notice, but he looks beyond the labels and sees who he made us to be: blameless and innocent; this is what he believes about you. These are his thoughts, his word about you.

> *"My thoughts," says the Lord, "are not like yours,*
> *and my ways are different from yours.*
> *As high as the heavens are above the earth,*
> *so high are my ways and thoughts above yours.*
>
> *"My word is like the snow and the rain*
> *that come down from the sky to water the earth.*
> *They make the crops grow...* [36]*

Just as the rain soaks into the ground and makes the crops grow, as we let his thoughts about us soak into our minds it will affect the way we think and act.

Activity

Draw some cartoon style pictures of your close friends then draw a label on them and write on each label a good quality you see in them.

Love is ...

...love is not happy with evil, but is happy with the truth. Love never gives up; and its faith, hope, and patience never fail. [37]

Jesus's demonstration of love for all kinds of people caused some people to get angry, for example in the story of Zaccheus, the people were grumbling when they saw Jesus kindness towards him. They probably thought Zaccheus didn't deserve kindness and couldn't understand what Jesus was doing, inviting him to tea.

How could Jesus love all people?

He did not delight in their evil but delighted in the truth about them. That they were created to be like God and are children of God.

Just like the father of the lost son, God never loses sight of the truth of who we are. God never gives up on us and always believes in us.

When the father ran to meet the son, with arms open wide to hug him, I'm sure the son couldn't help but hug back and enjoy his dad's love for him.

Knowing the truth, God's good opinion of us, is what sets us free. When we truly know his love, we respond, we love back!

I think the lyrics of the song 'fixer upper' from Disney's Frozen sum up this God kind of love well:

"We aren't saying you can change him
'Cause people don't really change
We're only saying that love's a force that's powerful and strange
People make bad choices if they're mad or scared or stressed

But throw a little love their way, and you'll bring out their
best
True love brings out the best."

Just like the theme in Frozen, it is only an act of true love that can help people overcome evil and bring them back to life.

Activity

Draw yourself under the banner.

His banner over me is Love

The Good Samaritan

This is love: not that we loved God, but that he loved us...[38]

Jesus meets a rich young man who asks: 'What must I do to receive eternal life?' In other words, how do I live right and be successful? Perhaps the man thought that he had done everything right, that he understood God because he had studied the Bible and learned all the rules about right and wrong. However the way that people thought about God, was often very different to how Jesus represented him and Jesus was the perfect example of God.

Jesus answers the rich young man by telling him a story of the Good Samaritan. The Jewish people of the day hated Samaritans, who were seen as outsiders, the enemy: people not to be mixed with and definitely not 'good'.

The story is another picture of God's kind of love.

Jesus answered, "There was once a man who was going down from Jerusalem to Jericho when robbers attacked him, stripped him, and beat him up, leaving him half dead. It so happened that a priest was going down that road; but when he saw the man, he walked on by on the other side. In the same way a Levite also came there, went over and looked at the man, and then walked on by on the other side. But a Samaritan who was traveling that way came upon the man, and when he saw him, his heart was filled with pity. He went over to him, poured oil and wine on his wounds and bandaged them; then he put the man on his own animal and took him to an inn, where he took care of him. The next day he took out two silver coins and gave them to the innkeeper. 'Take care of him,' he told the innkeeper, 'and when I come back this way, I will pay you whatever else you spend on him.'"

And Jesus concluded, "In your opinion, which one of these three acted like a neighbor toward the man attacked by the robbers?"

The teacher of the Law answered, "The one who was kind to him."

Jesus replied, "You go, then, and do the same." [39]

In this story the priests knew all the religious rules of right and wrong yet they didn't help the wounded man, who had been left for dead. The Samaritan was a supposed enemy of the man who'd been attacked, but it was only the Samaritan who would save, heal and bring him back to life. It was only an act of true love and kindness that could help the man.

The rich young man reminds me of myself growing up. I was only focused on what I thought I must do to please God. It was only as I discovered how much God loved me that loving others was no longer something I was expected to do, but more something I wanted to do; sharing the love that I receive from God. In telling this story Jesus shows that knowing God is not about keeping rules, but knowing how much you are loved.

Activity

Think about the difference between having to do something and wanting to do something and how it might affect the way you love others.

What About The Cross?

Your union with His death broke the association with that world; the secret of your life now is the fact that you are wrapped up with Christ in God. [40]

It was us who thought we were God's enemies but the truth is that he was always one with us.

Man's misunderstanding of God meant that many people didn't recognise Jesus as God's Son; this led to his rejection and eventually to his death. People were confused and upset when Jesus didn't turn out to be as they expected; so much so, that they plotted to kill him: an innocent man. Yet even in this awful event, only God's kind of love flowed from him; as Jesus died on the cross he forgave this awful crime against himself, saying *'Forgive them, Father. They don't know what they are doing.'*[41]

God saw that human beings were not acting as their true selves; they didn't know what they were doing because they had lost sight of who God had originally made them to be. They were trying to live right by their own rules but it only produced evil—so much that they killed Jesus.

But even at their worst, in this awful crime against Jesus, God used the death of Jesus to remind them of how loved and accepted they were, he forgave them and demonstrated that living right wasn't about finding who was to blame. Through Jesus's death he bought the old way of trying to live right to an end, and through raising Jesus from the dead, God confidently called out our original identity that he created in man from the very beginning. He brought us back to life!

For years man tried to find God, but it was always on man's own understanding, which was actually a misunderstanding of whom God really was. God was never far away or distant, he was never angry and unforgiving. He never left us. It was our understanding of God that got twisted and misshapen and left us lifeless. We tried to overcome evil by following certain rules and performing strange customs, but it was only when we were completely helpless that we were able to be rescued by life and love itself: God, who came to us as Jesus. We thought we were his enemy but he demonstrated his love for us and saved us—just as in the story of the Good Samaritan.

We are ruled by the love of Christ, now that we recognise that one man died for everyone, which means that they all share in his death. He died for all, so that those who live should no longer live for themselves, but only for him who died and was raised to life for their sake.

No longer, then, do we judge anyone by human standards. Even if at one time we judged Christ according to human standards, we no longer do so. Anyone who is joined to Christ is a new being; the old is gone, the new has come. All this is done by God, who through Christ changed us from enemies into his friends and gave us the task of making others his friends also. Our message is that God was making all human beings his friends through Christ. God did not keep an account of their sins, and he has given us the message that tells how he makes them his friends [42].

Activity

Fill in the missing vowels.

You're It. You're In!

*The kingdom of heaven is like treasure hidden in a field.
When a man found it, he hid it again, and then in his joy
went and sold all he had and bought that field.*

*Again, the kingdom of heaven is like a merchant looking for
fine pearls. When he found one of great value, he went away
and sold everything he had and bought it.*[43]

God's message to you is not one of: if you look a certain way or pass all the tests then you're in. No! God's message to you is the good news that you're already in! In him! Your life is hidden in Jesus. As you discover yourself, you'll find the treasure too.

When treasure gets buried in the ground, it might not look much like treasure, covered in layers of dirt but underneath the layers the original treasure is hidden. That treasure is like our true identity but sometimes it can get covered up, buried by the thoughts and beliefs we have about ourselves: thoughts of what or who we should look like; thoughts of trying to be like someone else, taking on others' opinions or styles, instead of being ourselves.

You are that treasure. You are that pearl! God made you to be like him and he has always had you in mind; you were always the centre of his attention. Your value and worth were so great to him that Jesus came to uncover the treasure that is you.

Long before he laid down earth's foundations, he had us in mind, had settled on us as the focus of his love, to be made whole and holy by his love. [44]

Spend a few minutes thinking about this, imagining how it feels to be accepted for who you are, imagine how much love and life you can bring to other people around you by accepting them as they are.

Activity

Doodle a cartoon of someone digging up some treasure in a field and how pleased they are to find it.

True Nature

Fix your thoughts on what is true and good and right. Think about things that are pure and lovely, and dwell on the fine, good things in others. Think about all you can praise God for and be glad about.[45]

When you were little your parents didn't explain to you how to talk or how to walk, you just saw your parents doing those things and copied them; the potential is within every healthy human being to do those things. When a little child learns to walk and talk it is something that happens naturally, without a lot of struggling. In fact it's often a lot of fun because Mum and Dad love to watch their children learning how to do these things, and give them lots of encouragement.

God designed you to live in these kinds of loving relationships and even though you might take after your parents or copy those around you, you are still uniquely yourself. You were created to connect with God and with others in this way.

I look at my own daughter growing up and I see how she sometimes reflects the likes and dislikes of her friend's. Just recently we were out walking with one of her friends, and as they ran ahead of me to scramble up a rock face I noticed how one had inspired the other to climb. They both wanted to climb the rock and because they felt comfortable around each other, they silently spurred each other on, and their enthusiasm was strengthened. I saw what a good connection they have and how they could truly be themselves in that moment.

In the same way, when you feel connected to God, and feel comfortable in his thoughts about you; that you are perfectly loved and accepted, your true nature is revealed. As you see the love and life God has for you, and discover it for yourself, it will change how you see life, yourself and how you see others.

You have so much potential within you, you were created to live life to the full, and you have so much to offer.

Activity

Write down a list of things you love to do with your friends. Then write down some things that you've never done but that you'd like to try.

Thank God for your friends and for his friendship with you.

Final Thoughts

If you live in me and what I say lives in you, then ask for anything you want, and it will be yours.[46]

Jesus once told a story about a farmer who went to sow some seed, some of the fell on the path, where people walked, and the seed got stepped on, and the birds came and ate them up. Some of the seed fell on rocky ground so even though the plant grew quickly it didn't take root and so dried up and died because it didn't have enough water. Some of the seed fell in with the weeds. As the plants grew, the weeds also grew and took over, and the seed couldn't get enough light. The other seed fell on good soil and when these plants grew they produced lots of fruit.

In this story the soil is like our understanding and the seed represents God's word.

Jesus told this story to show that things can stop us from believing what God says about us. Different things in life can distract us. Things people say or do, the things we see on the television or in magazines; even our own behaviour can make us doubt what God says. But when we begin to really understand who God is, through looking at Jesus, seeing the kind of close relationship he created us to be in with him, we believe he loves us, that he likes us, that he cares for us and we can enjoy a life of our dreams.

Did you know that what you spend your time thinking about shapes your whole life? So it's important to think about good things. You have an imagination that can be put to good use, some of the greatest inventors like Einstein and Leonardo Da Vinci were also great thinkers. So use your imagination well, there are so many things that you can see yourself being, the first step to living your dreams is dreaming them!

It was my hope and desire through writing this book, that it might help to water the seed sown in your life. That as you read this book, you will have lots of good thoughts to think upon, and that in discovering him, you discover you, because you are amazing, and you can do amazing things.

Bibliography

1. 1 Peter 1:23 (Good News Translation)

2. Ephesians 1:4 (GNT)

3. John 8:12 (New International Version)

4. John 1: 9–13 (The Message)

5. John 14:9 (NIV)

6. Luke 19:8 (GNT)

7. Mark 2:3–5

8. Romans 8:16 (GNT)

9. Psalm 34:8

10. John 1:18 (GNT)

11. Colossians 2:9–10 (New International Readers Version)

12. Luke 15:11-25 (GNT)

13. Luke 15:31 (GNT)

14. Luke 15:25–32 (GNT)

15. Psalm 100:3 (NIRV)

16. Proverbs 23:7 (King James Version)

17. Psalm 34:7 (English Standard Version)

18. John 19:26

19. Psalm 23:1–2 (NLT)

20. Philippians 4:6 (NLT)

21. Matthew 6:25–28 (NIRV)

22. Matthew 11:28 (NLT)

23. Ephesians 1:3–8 (GNT)

24. Luke 17:21 (God's word Translation)

25. Psalm 139:1–14 (GNT)

26. Psalm 139:14–18 (GNT)

27. 2 Corinthians 3:18 (NLT)

28. Isaiah 40:8 (NIV)

29. Deuteronomy 32:2 (GNT)

30. Acts 17:28 (GNT)

31. John 14:20 (GNT)

32. Isaiah 60:1 (NIV)

33. 1 John 4:18 (GNT)

32. 1 Corinthians 13:4–5 (GNT)

33. Zephaniah 3:17

34. Isaiah 55:8–10 (GNT)

35. 1 Corinthians 13: 6–7 (GNT)

36. 1 John 4:10 (NIV)

37. Luke 9:30–37 (GNT)

38. Colossians 3:2 (Mirror Translation)

39. Luke 23:34 (NIV)

40. 2 Corinthians 14–19 (GNT)

41. Matthew 13:44–46 (NIV)

42. Ephesians 1:3 (The Message)

43. Philippians 4:8 (Living Bible)

44. John 15:7 (God's word Translation)

45. Philippians 4:8 (Living Bible)

46. John 15:7 (God's word Translation)

Answers

Who is Jesus?

That God made his home in us

Holy Spirit

True, False, True, False

The Original Recipe

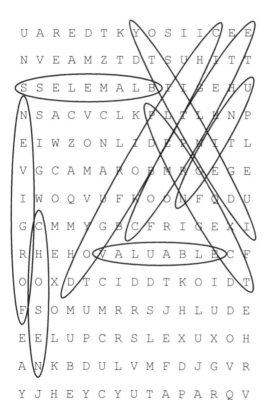

```
U A R E D T K Y O S I I C E E
N V E A M Z T D T S U H I T T
S S E L E M A L B I I E H U
N S A C V L K P L I H N P
E I W Z O N L I D E F I T L
V G C A M A R O B M R C E G E
I W O Q V U F K O O N F Q D U
G C M M Y G B C F R I G E X I
R H E H O V A L U A B L E C F
O O X D T C I D D T K O I D T
F S O M U M R R S J H L U D E
E E L U P C R S L E X U X O H
A N K B D U L V M F D J G V R
Y J H E Y C Y U T A P A R Q V
```

God is Not Distant

Blameless, Accepted, Loved, Valuable, Perfect, Child of God.

Reflect

Jesus shows me what I look like. I reflect him.

Lightning Source UK Ltd.
Milton Keynes UK
UKOW06f1453041215

264021UK00010B/196/P